The Ultimate
Ariana Grande
Fan Book

100+ Ariana Grande Facts,
Photos, Quizzes + More

Jamie Anderson

BELLANOVA

MELBOURNE · SOFIA · BERLIN

Copyright © 2022 by Jamie Anderson

The Ultimate Ariana Grande Fan Book 2022/23
www.bellanovabooks.com

All rights reserved. No part of this book may be reproduced in any form by any electronic or mechanical means including photocopying, recording, or information storage and retrieval without permission in writing from the author.

Ariana Grande was not involved in the writing of this book. However, all facts are believed to be truthful based on reputable, public domain sources.

Photos licensed by Shutterstock.com.
HARDCOVER
ISBN: 978-619-7695-53-3
Imprint: Bellanova Books

CONTENTS

Introduction	4
Ariana: Fun Facts	6
Ariana: The Quiz	26
Early Life	26
Music	34
Private Life	44
Everything Else	50
Ariana: The Lyrics Quiz	60
Ariana: Quotes	68
Word Search	78
Crossword Puzzle	80
Solutions	82
Join Us	84

Ariana Grande
INTRODUCTION

Welcome to **The Ultimate Ariana Grande Fan Book 2022/23**! As one of the most talented and inspiring artists in the world, Ariana has gone from strength to strength since she started out as Cat Valentine in 2009!

Now, Ariana has released six best-selling albums, and many chart-topping singles—*and* brought us four incredible tours. But we know there is still so much more to come from her!

So, are you ready to learn more about Ariana and test your knowledge? *Let's do this!*

—Jamie

Ariana Grande
FUN FACTS

Ariana loves going to the beach in the middle of the night. She finds it calming.

...

Ariana has really bad eyesight and wears contact lenses most of the time.

...

Despite being scared of heights, Ariana loves roller coasters and theme parks.

THE ULTIMATE ARIANA GRANDE FAN BOOK

Nothing burns more calories than dancing in 5-inch heels... try it!

— Ariana Grande

When Ariana's single with the Weeknd, *Save Your Tears*, reached number one—it was the sixth number one for both of them.

• • •

In 2019, Ariana had the first waxwork figure of her displayed at Madame Tussaud's in London, and fans helped to choose her outfit.

• • •

True Ariana Grande fans are called Arianators. However, they used to be called the Ariana Army and Tiny Elephants.

• • •

In 2022, a bottle of Ariana's fragrance, *Cloud*, was sold every 11 minutes at Ulta Beauty!

THE ULTIMATE ARIANA GRANDE FAN BOOK

Ariana Grande on the Sweetener World Tour at the O2 Arena in London on October 15, 2019.
Image: Batud1991

Ariana's beauty brand, r.e.m., was named Best New Brand at the 2022 *Allure Best of Beauty Awards*.

• • •

Ariana will play Glinda in the film adaptation of the musical *Wicked*. We can't wait to see it!

• • •

Ariana co-executive produced the soundtrack to the remake of *Charlie's Angels* in 2019. She sang the main track, *Don't Call Me Angel* with Miley Cyrus and Lana Del Rey.

• • •

Ariana loves reading books and is a huge fan of Harry Potter.

On her 29th birthday, in 2022, Ariana shared an adorable throwback video on Instagram of her as a child.

• • •

Ariana has never smoked a cigarette.

• • •

All of Ariana's full-length albums have gone platinum.

• • •

Ariana launched her first fragrance in September 2015, and since then she has sold over $750m of fragrances worldwide!

Ariana loves to sleep in as little clothing as possible. Her grandma taught her this.

・・・

Ariana has a major obsession with horror movies and has done since she was young.

・・・

One of Ariana's best friends, Jennette McCurdy, accidentally made Ariana's phone number public and later apologized.

At the age of ten, Grande co-founded the South Florida youth singing group *Kids Who Care*, which performed for charitable fundraising events, raising over $500,000 for charities in 2007 alone.

• • •

Ariana is a vegan, meaning she doesn't eat meat or animal products.

• • •

Ariana's favorite designer is Chanel.

• • •

Ariana's favorite subject is science.

Ariana's song, *Baby I*, was originally written for Beyoncé. Her song *Break Free* was written for Austin Mahone.

· · ·

Ariana is said to be worth over $220 million.

· · ·

Ariana's favorite foods are salmon and vegetables.

· · ·

Ariana's favorite perfume is Pink Sugar.

THE ULTIMATE ARIANA GRANDE FAN BOOK

Music is really driving my whole life.

— *Ariana Grande*

THE ULTIMATE ARIANA GRANDE FAN BOOK

Music is really driving my whole life.

— Ariana Grande

Ariana's favorite television shows are *Gossip Girl* and *Project Runway*.

• • •

Ariana used to be a cheerleader.

• • •

Ariana's TikTok account has 28 million followers (as of October 2022).

• • •

When she released *thank u, next* she broke the record for the largest streaming week for a pop album.

Ariana's mom thought she'd grow up to be a serial killer because she liked wearing Halloween masks.

・・・

Ariana has said that she loves animals more than she loves most people. This is partly why she is a vegan.

・・・

When Ariana is not wearing heels, she walks around on her tippy toes.

・・・

Ariana is hypoglycemic, meaning she has low blood sugar.

THE ULTIMATE ARIANA GRANDE FAN BOOK

Love your flaws, and own your quirks.

— *Ariana Grande*

At school one time, Ariana filmed her teacher shouting at her.

・・・

Ariana can make amazing impressions of celebrities including Celine Dion, Christina Aguilera and Jennifer Lawrence.

・・・

Ariana was the most-streamed artist of the decade on *Spotify* (2010-2020).

In 2013, Ariana was the opening act for Justin Bieber's *Believe* tour.

• • •

Ariana has a part in the 2021 Netflix film, *Don't Look Up*, starring Jennifer Lawrence.

• • •

Joan Grande, Ariana's mom, has had cameos in many of Ariana's music videos.

• • •

Although she isn't fluent, Ariana can speak quite good Italian. She even recorded a song in Italian with opera singer Andrea Boccelli.

Ariana Grande Quiz
EARLY LIFE

Can you answer these questions about Ariana from when she was younger?

The answers are at the end of the quiz.

1. Where did Ariana sing the national anthem when she was eight?

2. What age was Ariana when her parents got divorced?

3   When was Ariana born?

4   What is Ariana's full name?

5   Who was Ariana named after?

6   What was Ariana's first word?

7   Where did Ariana make her professional acting debut?

8   What are Ariana's parents' names?

9   What is Ariana's star sign?

10 What did Ariana collect when she was younger?

Plant love; grow peace.

— Ariana Grande

11   What was the first concert Ariana went to?

12   When did Ariana first start performing?

13   What schools did Ariana go to?

14   What was Ariana's favorite movie when she was very young?

15   How many siblings does Ariana have?

16   Which celebrity spotted Ariana singing on a cruise ship when she was 8 and said: *'You were meant to do this'*?

17   What was Ariana's character's full name in *Victorious*?

18 Which hockey team were her parents season ticket holders to when Ariana was a child?

19 Where was Ariana born?

20 What shoe size is Ariana?

21 How tall is Ariana?

22 Does Ariana have a middle name?

23 What was the first musical Ariana appeared in at her local theatre?

24 When did Ariana receive her high school diploma?

25 In which city did Ariana audition for Nickelodeon's *Victorious*?

ANSWERS

How many did you get right?

1. At a home game for the Florida Panthers.
2. Around 8 or 9
3. June 26, 1993
4. Ariana Grande-Butera.
5. Princess Oriana from Felix the Cat
6. "Bubble"
7. As Charlotte on the Broadway musical *13*, in 2008.
8. Joan and Edward
9. Cancer
10. Stuffed animals, hockey pucks and Halloween masks
11. Katy Perry in 2011
12. When she was eight.

13. Pine Crest School and North Broward Preparatory School
14. *The Wizard of Oz*
15. She has one half-brother called Frankie.
16. Gloria Estefan
17. Cat Valentine
18. Florida Panthers
19. Boca Raton, Florida
20. 7.5 US
21. 1.55m (5'0")
22. No
23. Annie
24. 2012
25. New York

THE ULTIMATE ARIANA GRANDE FAN BOOK

Ariana Grande Quiz
MUSIC & ACHIEVEMENTS

Now it's time to test your knowledge on Ariana's music and career.
Good luck!

1   What vocal range does Ariana have?

2   What is Ariana's signature stage outfit?

3   Name Ariana's six studio albums.

4   What does Ariana call her fans?

5   What Guinness World Record did Ariana break in 2022?

6   At what position on the Billboard charts did her album *Positions* debut?

7   How many awards was Ariana nominated for at the 2022 Billboard Music Awards?

8   How many singles has Ariana had on the Billboard Hot 100 (including collaborations)?

9   How long did it take Ariana to record her first album?

10 How many singles did Ariana release from her first album?

11 Ariana has a driver's license. True or false?

12 How many tattoos does Ariana have?

13 What was the name of the concert film Ariana released on Netflix in December 2020?

14 What was the name of Mariah Carey's Christmas song that Ariana rerecorded with Jennifer Hudson in 2020?

15 Who is Ariana's vocal coach?

THE ULTIMATE ARIANA GRANDE FAN BOOK

Everyone is beautiful, everyone is perfect, and everyone is lovely.

— Ariana Grande

16 How long did it take Ariana's debut album to reach #1 on iTunes?

17 How many Nickelodeon Kids' Choice Awards has Ariana won?

18 Ariana cried when she met which celebrity for the first time?

19 How many Guinness World Records has Ariana broken?

20 What was the name of the first single Ariana released from her *Positions* album?

21 Which of Ariana's fragrances was the best-selling fragrance at Ulta in 2022?

22 Who featured on Ariana's single *34+35*?

23 How many fragrances has Ariana released?

24 How many tracks are on her album *Positions*?

25 What is Ariana's official website URL?

26 What position did *Save Your Tears* reach on the Billboard Hot 100 chart?

27 Approximately how many Instagram followers does Ariana have as of October 2022?

28 Who did Ariana record the single *Save Your Tears* with?

ANSWERS

How many did you get right?

1. Four octaves, similar to Mariah Carey's.
2. Short skirts and crop tops with knee-high white boots.
3. *Yours Truly*; *My Everything*; *Dangerous Woman*; *Sweetener*; *thank u, next*; and *Positions*.
4. "My loves".
5. Most Nickelodeon Kids' Choice Awards blimps won for Favorite Female Artist.
6. Number one, of course!
7. Six.
8. 71
9. Three years
10. Five
11. True

12. 55
13. Excuse me, I love you.
14. Oh Santa!
15. Eric Vetro. He is also Katy Perry's vocal coach.
16. 15 minutes.
17. Nine.
18. Jim Carrey
19. 27
20. *Positions*
21. Cloud.
22. Doja Cat and Megan Thee Stallion
23. Eleven
24. 14 (19 on the deluxe edition)
25. www.arianagrande.com
26. Number one
27. 334 million
28. The Weeknd

Ariana Quiz
PRIVATE LIFE

What does Ariana get up to when she's not performing? Let's find out what you know!

1. How many pet dogs does Ariana have?

2. Can you name all of her dogs?

3. What other pets does Ariana have?

4. Who is Ariana married to?

5   Why does Ariana always wear her hair in a ponytail?

6   Who was Ariana's first celebrity crush?

7   Where does Ariana live?

8   Which fictional character has Ariana said she would marry?

9   What is Ariana's favorite type of footwear?

10 What is the name of Ariana's half-brother and best friend?

11 What type of food does Ariana eat every day?

12 Ariana and her ex, Big Sean, recorded two songs together. Can you name them?

13 How does she describe her ex, the late Mac Miller, in the track Thank U, Next?

14 What health problem does Ariana suffer from?

15 What religion was Ariana raised in?

16 In 2020, Ariana and her friends started an animal shelter in Los Angeles. What is it called?

17 What date did Ariana get married?

18 Who designed Ariana's wedding dress?

ANSWERS

How many did you get right?

1. Ten
2. Coco, Toulouse, Cinnamon, Strauss, Lafayette, Pignoli, Myron, Snape, Ophelia and Lily.
3. A pig
4. Dalton Gomez
5. Because she has bad hair loss from dyeing her hair red every week for her role in Victorious.
6. Justin Timberlake, when she was three.
7. Los Angeles
8. The Cookie Monster
9. Heels
10. Frankie
11. Strawberries. She eats at least five a day.
12. 2013's *Right There* and 2014's *Best Mistake*
13. As an 'angel'
14. Hypoglycemia
15. Roman catholic
16. Orange twins rescue
17. May 15, 2021
18. Vera Wang
19. Real estate agent

Ariana Grande Quiz
Everything Else

It's time for the random question round! Are you ready? Good luck!

1 What is Ariana's favorite color?

2 What is Ariana most afraid of?

I know that my fans will probably learn a lot about me by listening to my music, if they really listen to the lyrics.

— Ariana Grande

3   What is Ariana's favorite movie?

4   What was the theme for Ariana's 23rd birthday?

5   What does Ariana's mom do for a job?

6   In which 2020 movie does Ariana's brother Frankie play the character Richard?

7   What is Ariana's natural hair color?

8   On which cheek does Ariana have a dimple?

9 What is Ariana's favorite cereal?

10 What is Ariana's favorite animal?

11 Who is Ariana's favorite actress?

12 What are Ariana's nicknames?

13 On what TV show starring Jim Carrey did Ariana make a guest appearance in 2020?

14 What was the name of Ariana's 2019 tour?

15 Which Ben Stiller movie did Ariana cameo in?

16 Who are Ariana's main fashion inspirations?

17 What is Ariana allergic to?

18 Where does Ariana have a birthmark?

19 What languages can Ariana speak?

20 What is Ariana's favorite ice cream flavor?

21 What does Ariana's dad do for a job?

22 What was the color of Ariana's dress for her performance at the White House?

23 What religion does Ariana follow?

24 Why did Ariana abandon Catholicism?

25 Ariana had Vevo remove the video for her first single, *Put Your Hearts Up*. True or False?

Life is beautiful. Be thankful for everything.

— *Ariana*

26 Who were the opening acts of her *Sweetener* tour at the North American shows?

27 Which of Ariana's dogs makes a cameo in her *Positions* music video?

ANSWERS

How many did you get right?

1. Lavender
2. Lots of things! Heights, her hair falling out, damaging her vocal chords, and looking straight into the camera.
3. Bruce Almighty
4. Harry Potter
5. CEO at a communications company
6. Spree
7. Brown
8. The left cheek.
9. Cocoa puffs
10. Seahorse
11. Jennifer Garner
12. Riri, Ari and Little Cow

13. Kidding
14. Sweetener
15. Zoolander 2
16. Marilyn Monroe and Audrey Hepburn
17. Cats, bananas and dark chocolate
18. On her left shoulder/back
19. English and Spanish
20. Chocolate
21. He owns a graphic design firm in Florida
22. Black
23. Kaballah
24. It doesn't support LGBTQ+ rights
25. True
26. Normani and Social House
27. Toulouse

Ariana Grande
THE LYRICS QUIZ

How well do you know Ariana's music? It won't be easy, but you got this!

1. *It's the way you walk; The way you talk; The way you make me feel inside*

2. *I know I should've fought it; At least I'm being honest*

3 *'Cause it's my business, God as my witness*

4 *I used to be cautious; A little too reckless*

5 *Write my own checks like I write what I sing*

6 *One taught me love; One taught me patience*

7 *Said boy I'm tryna meet your mama on a Sunday*

8   *This is the part when I say I don't want ya; I'm stronger than I've been before*

9   *When I try to explain it I be sounding insane; The words don't ever come out right*

10 *I cried enough tears to see my own reflection in them*

11 *These friends keep talkin' way too much; Say I should give you up*

12 *I tell you all the things you should know; So, baby, take my hand, save your soul*

13 *I like the way you lick the bowl; Somehow your method touches my soul*

14 *Boy, you're such a dream if you can believe, ayy; Boy, you're such a dream to me*

15 *We got that jam, make them; Dance, make them lose their minds*

16 *Will I ever love the same way again?; Will I ever love somebody like the way I did you?*

17 *This is one small step for woman; One giant leap for woman-kind*

18 *Then I realize she's right there; And I'm at home like, "Damn, this ain't fair"*

19 *Right now, I'm in a state of mind I wanna be in, like, all the time*

ANSWERS

How many did you get right?

1. Daydreamin'
2. One Last Time
3. Dangerous Woman
4. Sometimes
5. 7 Rings
6. Thank u, next
7. Positions
8. Break Free
9. Baby I
10. My Everything

11. Side to side
12. God is a woman
13. Sweetener
14. R.E.M.
15. Higher
16. Off the table
17. NASA
18. Break up with your girlfriend, I'm bored
19. No tears left to cry

THE ULTIMATE ARIANA GRANDE FAN BOOK

Ariana Grande
QUOTES

Ariana is one of the coolest women we know, and she is always inspiring us with her quotes about life and love — both in real life and through her music.

Here are just a few of our favorite quotes from Ariana...

"Be happy with being you. Love your flaws. Own your quirks. And know that you are just as perfect as anyone else, exactly as you are."

• • •

"Some people will find any reason to hate. Don't waste your time. Lighten up! It takes so much less energy to smile than to hate. Enjoy life."

• • •

"If anyone tries to bully you don't let them. Take a positive energy, form a ball of rainbow power and just, like shove it."

"If you're passionate about something then it will definitely work out for you. You should never stop believing in something, and you shouldn't listen to anyone who tells you otherwise. Never give up on something you love."

...

"Take a load off, don't take everything so seriously. And just be happier."

...

"Destroy your ego. Free hugs. Sing your hearts out in the street. Rock 'n roll."

"The best fashion advice I'd say would be just to do what makes you comfortable and what makes you feel cute. And that's how you're gonna look your best. Because when you feel your best, everybody else can feel it too."

...

"I love my fans so much! I know I say it all the time, but I really appreciate all the things they have done for me."

...

"Love is a really scary thing, and you never know what's going to happen. It's one of the most beautiful things in life, but it's one of the most terrifying. It's *worth the fear because you have more knowledge, experience, you learn from people, and you have memories."*

• • •

"I'm so thankful for the internet because actors and singers and performers now have a way to connect with their fans on a very personal level which I think is quite special."

• • •

"One of the most terrible feelings in the world is knowing that someone else doesn't like you. Especially when you don't know what you've done to deserve it."

"Life is beautiful. Cherish every moment even if you're stressed or hurt or whatnot. There's always tomorrow and it always gets better."

...

"Don't ever doubt yourselves or waste a second of your life. It's too short, and you're too special."

...

"I don't regret any of the decisions I've made in my life. Because with every choice I've made, I've learned something new."

I love nerdy, cute, quirky boys who don't take themselves too seriously.

— Ariana Grande

When you feel your best, everybody else can feel it, too.

— Ariana Grande

"School is tough sometimes, but it's all about knowing who your real friends are."

• • •

"Block out all the negative energy, and just love."

• • •

"The best part about having true friends is that you can go months without seeing them and they'll still be there for you and act as if you'd never left!"

Ariana Grande
WORD SEARCH

```
W R A I N O N M E Q Z S
D H D R N K U H G D R A
S P O S I T I O N S H R
A S D H G F O N B Y T I
Z C A E F D N Y X Z H A
F L O R I D A R O C M N
G T R S I V C X Z U N A
H T D S B A L G S R F T
T H A N K U N E X T S O
N H G N J D S A G R D R
T E S W E E T E N E R S
R G R A M M Y S N B U P
```

Can you find all the words below in the word search puzzle on the left?

FLORIDA

THANK U NEXT

POSITIONS

ARIANA

RAIN ON ME

ARIANATORS

GRAMMYS

INTO YOU

SWEETENER

Ariana Grande

CROSSWORD PUZZLE

Answer the clues and fill in the crossword puzzle —good luck!

ACROSS

1. She has ten of them
3. First album
6. Star sign
7. Song with Justin Bieber
8. Birth month

DOWN

1. Husband's first name
2. 2020 album
4. Birth town
5. Brothers name

THE ULTIMATE ARIANA GRANDE FAN BOOK

PUZZLE SOLUTIONS

		R	A	I	N	O	N	M	E		
					N						A
		P	O	S	I	T	I	O	N	S		R
						O						I
			A					Y				A
	F	L	O	R	I	D	A		O			N
				I					U			A
						A						T
	T	H	A	N	K	U	N	E	X	T		O
							A					R
			S	W	E	E	T	E	N	E	R	S
			G	R	A	M	M	Y	S			

We hope you learnt some awesome facts about Ariana! Feel free to leave us a review—it always makes us smile :)

And visit us at
www.bellanovabooks.com
for monthly book giveaways and more!

www.ingramcontent.com/pod-product-compliance
Lightning Source LLC
LaVergne TN
LVHW021332080526
838202LV00003B/144